The Runaway Piglet

Julie Patterson

Author / Illustrator of "Peggy's Day on the Farm (2021), Josh's New Skateboard (2022), Horrie the Horrible (2023), Why do Ants Bite? (2023).

Julie Patterson was born in Brisbane, Queensland and grew up in Sale Victoria, Australia. She grew up with her mum, stepdad and two brothers - one older and one younger. Julie met her sisters from her dad's side of the family as an adult, as she was her dad's youngest child of five daughters. Julie enjoys writing children's books, then in-turn illustrating them, visualising her pictures as she writes.

After many years of working in the banking and finance industry, Julie changed direction in her career to the corrections / justice industry. She remains happily married and strives to have multiple books published.

Copyright: © Julie D. Patterson (2023)

The rights of Julie D. Patterson, is to be identified as author and illustrator of this work.
This work is copyright. Apart from any use permitted under the Copyright Act 1968, no part may be reproduced by any process, nor may any other exclusive right be exercised, without the permission of Julie D. Patterson P.O. Box 207 Traralgon, Vic. 3844. (2023) All rights reserved.
You may find a catalogue record of this title in the Australian National Library.
ISBN : 978-1-923054-08-0 (Paperback)
ISBN : 978-1-923054-09-7 (eBook)

Julie D. Patterson
P.O. Box 207
Traralgon Vic 3844
Australia

The Runaway Piglet

Julie Patterson

This book belongs to:

....

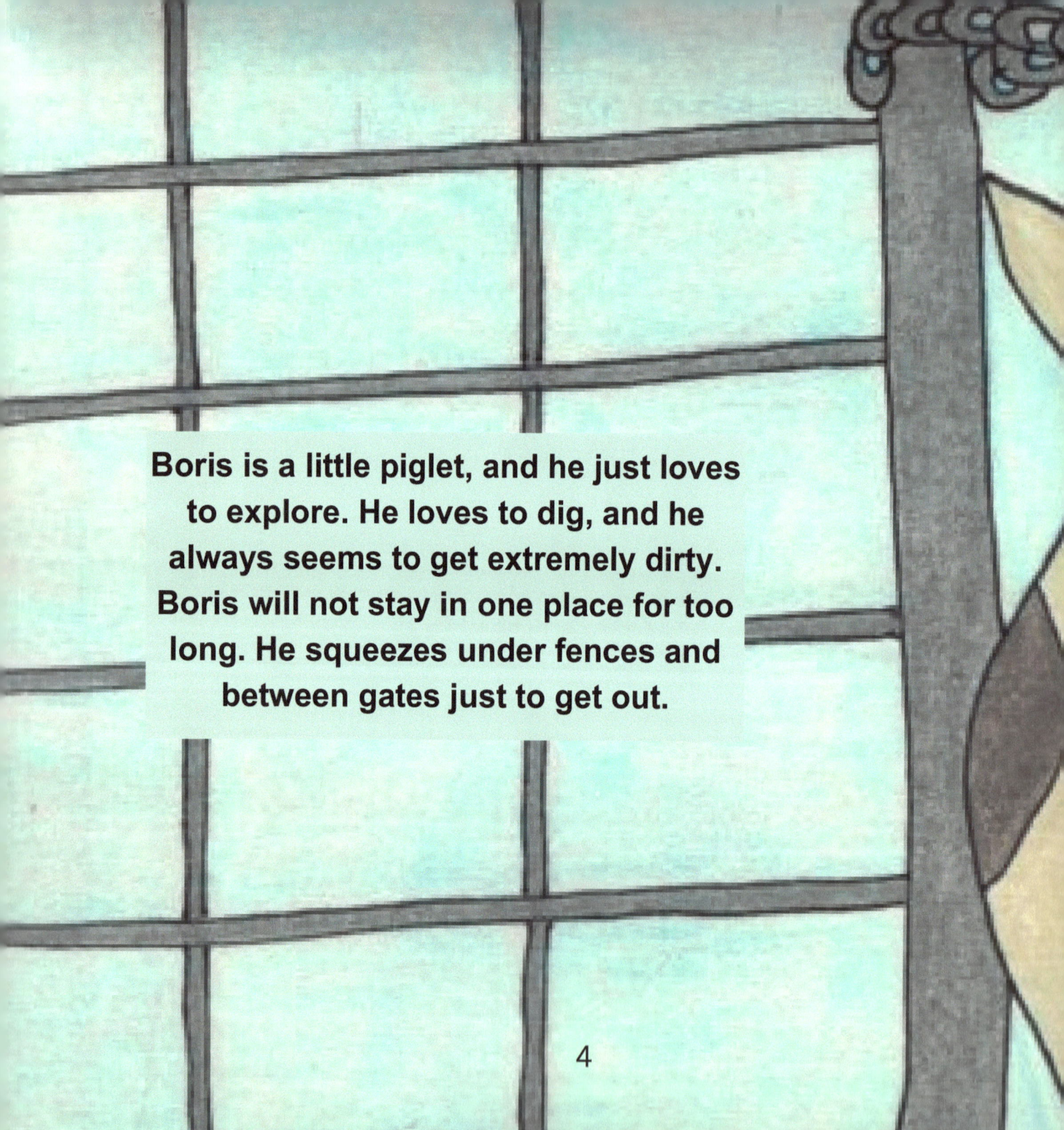

Boris is a little piglet, and he just loves to explore. He loves to dig, and he always seems to get extremely dirty. Boris will not stay in one place for too long. He squeezes under fences and between gates just to get out.

Boris enjoys the smell of flowers, when simply, out of haste, he digs to uproot them. Recently Boris dug up an entire field of daisies when, "OUCH!" Boris got stung on the top of his nose by an angry bee. That really hurt!

Boris stayed there for a couple of days until he worked out how to escape. He jumped at the opportunity to run through the legs of a worker feeding the animals.

Boris heard some music and laughter of workers building a new shed and he thought he would go over there to explore what was going on. Boris was sniffing around and he found some food. He worked out how to lift the lid on the lunch box. Yippee! Food Yum! Yum! Boris devoured a thickly spread, gooey peanut butter sandwich. Crunch! Crunch! The apple was gone! Then he ate the cherries. Spit! Spat! Out came the seeds.

14

Last of all, he came across a noisy square packet and couldn't work out how to open it. Boris sat on the packet when it let out a loud pop! It was a packet of chips, and they were very crunchy. Crunch! Crunch! Crunch! And they were all gone. They were quite salty, delicious and noisy to eat. Angry workers discovered what Boris had done and shooed him away. Their lunch was now gone! The workers showed extreme horror.

Oh well! Boris merrily wandered away. As for Boris, he could not see what the big deal was. He went off, exploring through the trees and bushes. When he turned around, he saw a blue tongue lizard. He said hello to the lizard, and he wondered why the lizard was being cheeky, poking out his beautiful blue tongue.
A hare startled Boris. Gee they can move! This long-eared critter darted from one side of Boris to the other.

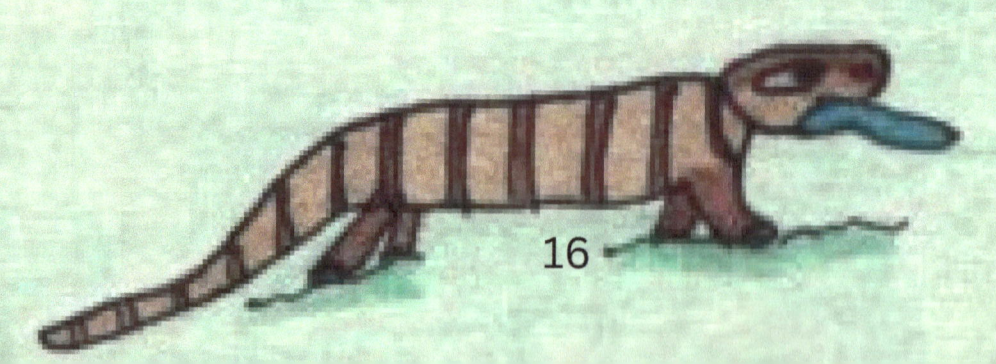

Feeling extremely thirsty, Boris went by a billabong to have a drink. Suddenly out jumped a frog rib bit! Rib bit! The frog was a noisy little fellow. He watched him jump back into the water and vanish.

There was a noise coming from a garden, and Boris went to check it out. It was a lady singing while pruning her plants in her garden. She opened the gate to take her cuttings down to the side paddock when Boris took the opportunity and ran into her yard. The lady picked up Boris to move him on and he let out an ear-piercing squeal. The lady put him down and he ran back again. Again, Boris squealed when she touched him. He clearly did not like being held.

She grabbed her broom and shooed him away. Boris took the hint when she smacked him on the bottom with the broom and he wondered off again.

Boris was strolling along when he saw familiar surroundings. Wow! He had made it back home again to his brothers and sisters. Boris's mum and dad were very grumpy when he arrived home and they demanded to know where he had been. Boris filled them all in on his little adventure. Boris had a good feed of slops that night and slept very well as he was back home again. Ah! There is no place like home!

The End